Published by Christian Focus Publications Ltd
Geanies House, Fearn, Tain, Ross-shire IV20 1TW www.christianfocus.com

Copyright © John Brown Brian Wright
ISBN: 978-1-5271-1168-4

This edition published in 2024
Cover illustration and internal illustrations by Lisa Flanagan
Cover and internal design by Lisa Flanagan
Printed and bound by Imprint, India

Hosea

& God's Love

John Brown
Brian Wright

UZZIAH   JOTHAM   AHAZ

Two centuries after King David died,
during the reigns of five well-known kings in Judah
and Israel, there lived a kind man named **Hosea**.

One day God gave Hosea **an unusual mission**,
a unique mission never given before or since.

Hosea was to show the people of Israel **the depth of God's love** by marrying an unfaithful woman named Gomer, who disobeyed God and wandered from His righteous path.

"Take Gomer", a woman with a wandering heart,
Whose choices have torn her world apart;
Marry her, Hosea, and love her strong;
Show my people where they've gone wrong."

Hosea obeyed God's odd command and married Gomer, promising to love her without end.

Their life together started off well,
and **Gomer soon bore him a son.**

But despite God's blessings,
Gomer again disobeyed and wandered away.

She began to make choices that **hurt Hosea deeply**,
leaving him heartbroken and upset.

Indeed, Gomer was a bad wife and an unfaithful woman. **She broke her marriage VOWS** to stay faithful to Hosea and looked for love instead with other men from other nations who worshiped other gods.

Israel had done the same thing with God.
They broke their vows to stay
faithful and turned to other gods instead.

Yet, even with all the pain and unfaithfulness,
Hosea's love for Gomer never stopped—
just like God's love for His people never stops.

Hosea continued to care for Gomer,
showing her grace and forgiveness even in the face
of difficult circumstances.

As **Gomer's choices led her further away** from Hosea and her family, she found herself in a very, very bad place.

But at just the right moment,
**Hosea extended his hand of love
and RESCUED her**. He paid off all her
debts to set her free from her troubles.

Hosea's loving act of buying Gomer back
was a powerful reflection of
God's never-ending love for His people.

Just as **Gomer** gave Hosea's goods to other men,
Israel had taken God's gifts—like grain to eat,
wine to drink, oil to bathe in, and silver and gold to
spend—and used them to serve false gods.

Just as **Gomer** was ungrateful and unfaithful to Hosea, **Israel** was ungrateful and unfaithful to God.

And just as **Gomer's** sin led to suffering and slavery, so did **Israel's** sin.

Yet, Hosea rescued and restored **Gomer**, just like God would do for **Israel.**

"Your sin has separated you from Me,
but if you **return to Me**,
I will return to you," said the Lord.

"Indeed, when My people return and rededicate themselves to Me, I will restore them and bless them through **a king from David's line.**"

Hosea was telling the people that a **descendent of King David** would come and reign.

This **promised Messiah** would be the true heir to the throne of David and the rightful king of all Israel. He alone would save and unite all God's people —**Jews and Gentiles**— forever as they commit themselves fully to Him as their King.

In response to His **great plan of salvation,**
God called the people to properly acknowledge
Him through true acts of worship.

For God told them, "Don't be like the morning clouds that look like they will rain but never do. **Don't pretend as if you will love and obey Me** but then act unfaithfully. Believe Me, your guilt and shame will not go away with time."

"Don't be like a **half-baked cake**
—disgusting and useless."

"Don't be like **a bird without brains**
—threatened and defenseless."

Although Israel had learned not to worship idols, **they never returned and committed themselves** fully "to the Lord their God and David their king."

This Davidic King was none other than **King Jesus**, who is coming again to reign over all the earth.

Therefore, we await Jesus' second coming —when He returns to earth.

Until then, the story of Hosea
teaches us that
**love is not just a
feeling,**
it is a choice,
a commitment,
and a reflection of who God is.

Just like Gomer, we have been given
**the opportunity to be
rescued from our sin**
if we would turn and commit
ourselves fully to the Lord our God
and Jesus our King.

No matter how many mistakes you've made,
you are never beyond the reach of God's never-ending love and grace,
which are only found in Jesus Christ.

"Whoever is wise,
let him understand these things
—for **the ways of the Lord
are right.**"

Christian Focus Publications publishes books for adults and children under its four main imprints: Christian Focus, CF4K, Mentor, and Christian Heritage. Our books reflect our conviction that God's Word is reliable and that Jesus is the way to know Him, and live for ever with Him.

Our children's publication list covers pre-school to early teens. We also publish personal and family devotionals, biographies and inspirational stories that children will love.

From pre-school board books to teenage apologetics, we have it covered!

Christian Focus Publications Ltd,
Geanies House, Fearn, Ross-shire,
IV20 1TW, Scotland,
United Kingdom.
www.christianfocus.com

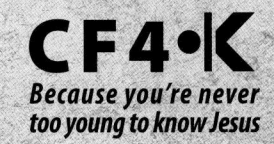

CF4•K

*Because you're never
too young to know Jesus*